Bright Scarves of Hours

Bright Scarves of Hours

Diane Tucker

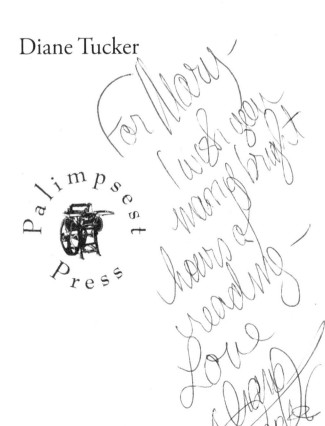

Palimpsest Press

Palimpsest Press
96 Stewart St, Kingsville, Ontario, Canada N9Y 1X4
www.palimpsestpress.ca

Typeset in Garamond & Zapfino
Printed and bound in Canada on recycled paper
Typesetting & design: Dawn Kresan
Author photograph: Joe Tucker

Library and Archives Canada Cataloguing in Publication

Tucker, Diane L. (Diane Lynne), 1965-
Bright scarves of hours / Diane Tucker.

Poems.
ISBN 978-0-9733952-7-3

I. Title.

PS8589.U28B74 2007   C811'.54   C2007-903082-3

Versions of these poems have appeared in *The Dalhousie Review, Astropoetica, Gumball Poetry, Another Toronto Quarterly, Crux: the Regent College Journal, paperplates, Jones Av, SPIRE, the poetry poster, Quills Canadian Poetry Magazine, The 13th Warrior Review, www.latchkey.net, Green's Magazine, The Aurora Review, Absinthe Literary Review, RUMINATE: faith in literature and art, The Vancouver Review,* and in the anthology *From this new world* (TenDollar Words Publishing 2003).

Bright Scarves of Hours

THE HOURS' PROLOGUE

9 A.M. DROP THE CHILDREN OFF AT SCHOOL, REMEMBERING

10 A.M. SORT THE VACATION SNAPSHOTS

11 A.M. CALLS

1 P.M. LETTERS

2 P.M. WALK THE DOG

3 P.M. BRING THE CHILDREN HOME FROM SCHOOL

5 P.M. MAKE DINNER WHILE LOOKING FORWARD TO THE WEEKEND

6 P.M. GREET SPOUSE ARRIVING HOME FROM WORK

7 P.M. GO OUT. COME HOME

THE HOURS' EPILOGUE

The Hours' Prologue

writers in autumn

We're done with heady summer,
with growth and fruitfulness
and the stress of keeping our cool.

Now we all, like trees, retreat, pull back,
shut down, withdraw the chlorophyll,
let our green leaves die and sail away.

We stand silent as the bark chills,
sap slows, as if a tree could look at you
with drowsy relief, with heavy-lidded eyes.

The leaves we drop are words,
brown ones mostly, the odd dull gold
and hopefully a scarlet one or two.

But they'll all be fragile, short-lived,
sere and crisp; listen carefully
before you move and they crumble in your hand.

9 a.m. Drop the children off at school, remembering

yellow vinyl 1972

Seven-year-old hands on the arborite kitchen table
still and spread, being heated by the sun
which is plastered thick as yellow vinyl,
green kitchen radio plays an Arlo Guthrie song:

Good mornin' America how are ya?

It's a train song, filling up the empty kitchen
and it makes me want to be in America
where the sun falls dry as yellow wheat straws
and the sunbeams fill with dust on the running rails

I know my daddy drives a truck to America
and I want to imagine he is in that song
his truck goes everywhere and the singer knows
my daddy is the Driver of America

hey don't you know me? I'm your native son

on my small hot hands against the arborite
the sun is yellow vinyl
Daddy is somewhere in his truck in America

I'll be gone five hundred miles when the day is done

the ditch in the lane

As a child they could not keep me from wells…
        Seamus Heaney, "Personal Helicon"

everything small — grass blade scale
mouse words: a hidden world, a history
long and narrow, deeper than the ditch

in that cool emerald wetness
my little self believed in all small beings
pixies, fairies bending every blade
I searched and searched the grass
and slow water, while it clasped my heart:
the longing to be *small*

to befriend all things mouse-sized
and silent, to sail away on the ditch
water that for fairies would be clean
it was so black, and cold as jewels

to drink it would have been
to become what it was — pure
strong movement, all my limbs
shifting grass and sticks aside
in a flowing as sure as the song
pushing out of a singing bird

surely I prayed to be made one
of that world, to be overpowered
by greens so glassy and wet-sweet
you had to eat and drink them,
to become a pixie with no other task
than to disappear from human eyes
amid the grass

hydrangea

The hydrangea bush, pursuing
its pale blue life in my parents' front yard,
my father would prune every year
to a hedgehog simulacrum — a mound
of naked beige sticks bristling the air,
sticks marble-smooth and filled with
wonders! — God's own styrofoam.
In January they made sharp, frozen *snaps*.

But every summer the hydrangea grew vast,
round and green-blue in our faces,
obscured the old tire it was planted in,
opened its broad leaves like happy hands
and held out its bundles of humble flowers:
watery blue, each small flat blossom
beaming, finding strength in numbers.

Grandma would cut some, put them in vases,
and those smooth foamy sticks could take it, I knew
because every year they passed the strictest test:
my father with his pruning shears
and me, thinking him ham-fisted and harsh.

But that's what years are for, for learning
that your father gave the round hydrangea bush
the greatest love it ever knew, reducing it
to the nub of itself each winter, conserving
in its roots, in the earth, all its spreading blue.

birthday kiss

Jericho Beach a place of sunset spells — coral sky and the constant breeze, waves stroking the shore, sweeping sand at us, waving.

Sunlight dusk-stained orange paints faces with a glaze of truth-telling. I'll believe whatever you tell me here, anything that comes out of your golden-halo mouth.

I'll believe in the sanctity of sitting on the sand, of saying sorry, of offering up a birthday kiss, brief and sweet as the last bite of the Last Supper.

After that you can smile all you want, sweetheart. Say anything. Squeeze me into the car on your lap; use me as a seatbelt all the way home.

You planted a kiss and there's no stopping it — what's planted grows.

What you planted as goodbye is really just a burial of what will push itself up inexorably: a poisonous flower, sunset-coloured, that will bloom and bloom.

failed actress

Damn art. She wants merely to haunt them,
      live in their heads that false eternity
of muse, star, goddess. Oh, that they'd leave home
      to follow her, to feel her touch, their sad
eyes fixed on hers, hands trembling on her skin.

She is a decorated *papier mâché* girl,
      a hot piñata full of candy — she wants them
to hit her hard enough to break her open.
      She wants to spill her sweet guts out and see
them scrabble on the ground for bits of her.

10 a.m. Sort the vacation snapshots

dragonflies

jewel shards in flight, the breath
of amethysts manifest over green glass
dexterously mating in the iridescent air

a tenderness of perfect narrow machinery

shimmering over the lake, wingtips
slice the heart's sealed chambers
shake vision free for a bright instant:

shot-silk arrows

at the lake, reading "The Wreck of the Deutschland"

sun on the shining, spattered shoulders

lake water splashes on the page

as the seas rage
   swallow priest and nuns
   with a wet wave-smack

the kids on the dock fling themselves into it
that swallowing water, they seek it,
one hunger meeting another with grasping fingers
sleek swimsuits
hair glistening on the sparkled surface

and on the wet nuns, nuns
drowning in my lap
Christ, their albatross, seeming-dead
against the mast

God's water is hands
   God's water dandles one and tears another
    and is water still and we love it

enough to give our children to it
   though Christ's sailors and lily ladies
    are sucked into its black and silver belly

bear love

salmon spine
curved into a C among the river rocks
like a bleached fern frond
a huge naked feather
like a bear's quill pen

the bear writes on river rocks
on salmon skulls
the bear sucks the bones dry

and uses the great white quills
to write love songs to the river
songs of unrequited gratitude for fish
songs written in salmon blood

the bear can't keep the songs in
he must make the quill sing for him
he hurls the rocks, the skulls, into the river
into his deaf lover's lap
where they're washed away with no reply

he sees another fish and his thoughts
turn bloody, but his belly's not empty

the bear hunts for love songs
the bear needs more ink

boomerang experiment

The early Universe is full of sound waves compressing and rarefying matter and light, much like sound waves compress and rarefy air inside a flute or trumpet.
    Paolo De Bernardis, astronomer

You felt the quivering heft of it in your hands and cherished every sprung quark, each atom compressed to life by your holy kisses, the universe a living .zip file ready to fly open.

In a six days' arc you flung it, your tensed arms and throat a song, the aboriginal Song, pushed by your initial breath into every electron, the very keening desire of Love the invisible waves pushing it all apart, showing it how far it could go.

But this is the Boomerang experiment. You fling the finely honed bent wing — all the matter Spirit can sing forth — into its own happening, its own spread thin thousand thousand ending, because you know the inevitable snap-back; the eventual pulsing of the song that will play back along itself.

It is the theme of this music: before you can find you must lose; you must exhale to get your breath back as music; you must send harmony swinging through the spheres before the chords come home.

"The new results are from a new, more detailed, analysis of images obtained by the Boomerang (Balloon Observations of Millimetric Extragalactic Radiation and Geophysics) experiment. "
    David Whitehouse, BBC News Online science editor

releasing the energy in the wood

sunlight, water, minerals
gathered atom by atom through the silent leaves
the deep invisible roots

for a hundred years? two?
and with one bundle-shouldered swing of the axe
the gathering begins to be a scattering

the compacted life severed, blocked,
chipped and stacked to dry

the sticks then placed over kindling like a stook
a teepee, a house for flame

and once more a trigger, a release, the rough stroke
of a match, its tiny snap-flame
nested in the wooden house's hearth

and without a breath, a word
the release is gained, the door
of solid matter flung wide with a grey trail
and the wood is freed to be flame, to be heat

to cover our faces with night-paint
our spread hands with this ancient, borrowed sunlight
concentrated into night to cheat the moon

then fall finally into embers like the original:
steam, carbon, and a red field of imparted starlight

it flares; its gases fight
and dance across its molten surface
and the furnace of time and space
is in miniature for our late eyes – the first heat,
unalloyed, that filled the skies but did not burn God's hand

oliver aurora

too far south
yet given grandly
this August desert night

the moon rises
and skeins of narrow veils
rush ghostly up the sky
to meet her, rising
with coyote calls

a breath-white wing opens
pinioned rhythm, rising

and a starship then
saucer shape
of smudged silver light
bleeds through black
above the line of mountains

veils, wing, receding ship:
the sky swathes, reaches
sails away

strikes you staring, standless
as if you'd been lifted, dandled
in a moonbright hand

summer's end

summer's end is hiding near the pool
disguising himself in chlorine smells
and warm breezes, but cannot help
but lift his nose into the air
while the children cannonball
(their phosphorescent flippers
flames in the chemical blue)

summer is their wet hair, dripping
over goggle straps, their shoulders brown
and peeling, and summer's end
is loath to lose them, wants their feet
forever dusty and sandal-shod

so he skulks, nosing down old lanes
in the cooler middle of the night
whispers *August* very slowly
and won't pronounce *September*
until Labour Day, when his last words
are new school shoes and early sundowns
waves of chill and the looming equinox

By this time the summer's got himself a periscope and can see round the corner.

See the hummock of September, a golden hill deceptively gentle in the distance, its far side dropping off into dry leaves and darkness.

Relieved only by a small plateau, October, set high enough (and carpeted with moss) to see the last horizontal sun, a deep and waxy orange light on the backs of hands.

Until November, all those dead leaves again, and mere dampness. Ahead another curve, and no light.

But by this time summer's got himself a periscope, and round the corner thinks he sees an unbroken yellow season.

november 28: in the shower

Still have the tan lines
from August's camping trip.

Burn lines, really, from when the sun
finger-painted red our backs and shoulders
and it felt like this shower, like the water
as hot as I can stand it pounding my back.

When I get out of the shower
it will be like when the sun dipped behind the trees
and the chill fell — all of us diving into tents
for jeans and sweatshirts.
The only burning then being watery instant cocoa
against our tongues and the popcorn
a foil moon swelling in its inflatable pan.

But I'm still in the shower, thinking now
of the midnights, the four of us drowsy
yet driven to stay up and swallow every second
of a sky so star-loaded it was sure to fall on us.
Fear as big as anything I could imagine
smothered me as we stood, staring and slack-jawed:
surely no one I thought *is allowed to be this happy.*

Now I turn and let hot water
pound on my breastbone. I close my eyes
so everything is black; squish my eyelids
so golden sparks fly all across the blackness
and feel, while my back and legs grow cold,
a heat concentrate around my heart. Yes.

Midnight, camping in August, was like that.

11 a.m. Calls

while praying

the sound of limbs
moving through bath water
the little waves invisible
a cleansing music
from behind the closed door

the sound of a wet body
squeaking against the tub
as I pray for our encrusted skin:
years of dark build-up on the soul

the water swirling now, echoing in the pipes
the bather is done, has begun dressing

my bed of prayer is a clean boat floating
here on the muddy side of the door

door

Stop being that brilliant door.

I hate every golden inch
of the scented wood of which you're made.

All your shining hinges should be broken
and left in the rain to rust.

Your leaded window is dark:
the colours of blood and midnight.

If only your lock were less intricate
or received a key I could possibly possess.

But then I'd have to grasp your
well-wrought silver handle and I'd hate that.

I'd have to hold it tight
and long enough to swing you wide.

And then I'd have to let you go.
And then I'd have to pass through.

immersion

you're actually waiting for it now
not distracting yourself
with sunlight and azure shadows
but anticipating being dragged
to your depths
bracing yourself, contemplating
the deeper shades
of blue you'll be forced to breathe
letting your thoughts rest
as long as you dare let them
on the chill and thickening darkness

ninety percent of you
underwater, you're that iceberg
waiting for the Titanic
to graze your side

you're that blundering ship
watching, but too late,
your whole heart rise up
snap in two
descend into its hypothermic daze

just enough consciousness to ask:
is it better to be rescued?
is it better to be drowned?

or is there in fact rescue
at the bottom of the berg
when you've gone as deep
as you can go
when heat is a memory
light become a myth
when you're frozen, blue-blind
in the water that doesn't end?

better yet

outside portholes on either side
of your head: God

filling the view for a minute: ocean
foam washing the decks
capsize imminent

then all you see: sky
flat, grey, a tarp
waterproofing nothing

after several years of this rolling
you think it's time
to venture out on deck, approach
the rail, feel for yourself the actual play
of spray and sky
be wave-spattered

better yet set out in a lifeboat
abandon ship

better yet let the ocean have you
by now you're soaked
the sky just a moist breath
between dives

better yet say *I'm a fish*

better yet
drown

rain: reunion

Will you brave this rain and visit me?
We'll sweep aside his curtain when you come,
but leave his muted music on the roof.
Each drop a fall, each fall a beat, a note
with which the rain continually composes
his song of splash and spread, of striking home.

Won't you come and hear it? Your presence
is all the rain needs to begin his song.
An audience, ensconced in this dry house
with time and coffee cups, is all he needs
to crank the volume of his love's wet music.

We'll talk, of course, summer as our theme,
when getting wet was everything we longed for,
the air an oven, our skin its dusty bread.
Rain will interrupt: "*That's why I've come.
You waited, parched. You prayed, you longed for me.*"

Won't you deign to come to rain's reunion?
His song is true — although we cower inside
it's him we want, and now his silver kisses
seek us, blown and spattered down the windows.
His music fills us up. We're swollen rivers.
Burst your banks and meet me where he falls.

1 p.m. Letters

after the reading

went home and read you
until after midnight

listened to *Great Big Sea*
sing about turning — listened
to the whistle, drums and keening song
until the eastern ocean spilled out my eyes

said too late, too late
for fish and rocks absent in the black
windy night, for space falling
dashing itself open

speaking is over
reading is over
night is just beginning

absence

If we love, what we love disappears, the one we love a centre
that cannot stay...
            Russell Thornton, "One Single Bread"

my silence is my love; my absence
the truest word of love that I can utter

the space my body does not occupy
is as close to you as love can carry me

words of love that, said, would crack your heart
are words locked up, hiding in my throat

a gaze that's never held —
a pair of eyes stuffed blind with looking love

disease untreated is my love, a pain
egged on, a sickness long pursued

the more I love the smaller it appears
compacted like a bullet in my brain

hitting at light speed when I least expect it
it takes me softly, dying while I live

unhad, untouched, unknown
but not unloved

gaze

your own eyes did it,
though they tried to slide back
into your secret comfortable skull

while I tried to pin them, tried
to nail your gaze

I can't remember now
how your mouth looked
it was a pair of eyes I was after

two dark doors to chutes
falling into your quivering chest

a time or two they opened enough
for a few bright birds to escape
and fly to me

I took them in, gave them safety
a place to nest and feed

open your dark eyes
and set more free

praying for the organist

last night I heard Fauré through a flute and prayed for you
I was thinking of your arms, your bare forearms over the piano keys
thick as sailor's arms, the hands fleshy starfish reaching
for each key with the surety of creatures landing on their native rock

the roundness of your worship, its buttoned, talc-dry athleticism
such a strength stretched gymnast-like against the walls of the music
every breath, stress, step, aimed out, up, through the pipes, yes,
but up also out of us

this gift, this knack of being a living spiritual contagion
an energy-white hum of praise

your fingers, ivory now through and through, grow tendrils
into the keys, whole seasons burgeoning under them measure by measure
they are the very sound of the first psalm, that tree by the streams of water
bearing   unwithering

I will miss singing psalms under your hand
how each became sculptural, like a pot, spinning, fingered into life
on the wheel — the clay moving in and out, up, tapering to a nothingness
how you exhorted us to sing like sculptors, to breathe beauty, to embody it
like Fauré through a flute

like when it all came down to your forearms over the piano keys
how I couldn't stop watching you play; how I had to look away; pretend to pray

how many nights

How many nights are remembered
because of who was not there?
The shadow you waited to see obscuring
the porch light, the shoulders shifting
as they'd reach for the bell, the knob; knowing
that you were wanted, had been stopped for,
that someone had put aside hours
to be with you.
This was what you did not have
and you remember.

It's all so innocent —
we all have our own lives, and being
in the same room with certain people
            is a tremor too eagerly sought.
And we so easily frighten one another;
            young rabbits afraid to be eaten.
You understand this: it's true; it's reasonable.
            But that doesn't untwist your stomach
when the door, opened, lets in just cold air.

semi-precious

like one of those plants
that stretches underground
and sprouts in another place

I wonder where you'll turn up, and when
and what words I'll save
to give you when you appear

they could be silver words, polished
like a fine chrome fender
but you'd see past those in a minute

semi-precious words, then, jade
or malachite, green words for you
to wear cool against your neck

and words of polished wood
plant flesh, fine-grained, sanded
and oiled, dense and rich as hazelnuts

I'll sew a special pocket for this
present of tumbled and polished words
keep them in handfuls on my hip

keep walking through the same wood
on the path surrounded by the dark vine
running close to the ground

where over the blade-leafed vine
bleeding hearts crowd, blooming
chances are one of them will be you

my book in your bag

if I were my book

if I were in your luggage   thumping against your hip

my hands in your hair   uncovering your ears   looking for your eyes

during the flight my folded body   would be hidden
under the seat

I don't come out   while you're in the sky
I don't come out   in the airport lounge

you save me   for the hotel room

the faceless chairs empty closet   unslept sheets

you can take me out of your bag   crack my spine

my lines   will tie you to the mattress
press your cover and mine together   perfect bound

I'll tear you open as though   you were a fresh brick of cherry bombs

all the words in me   gathering up your broken body

going

Stars, I let you go.
Don't stand in formation for me.
Retire below the horizon.

Moon, don't come when I call.
Don't take any more of my
mooncalf guff. I know you're not
my private singing telegram.

Rain, dry up out of my head.
Rebuke, refuse me
when I try to invoke what you are.
I'm not your poet laureate.

Everyone in earshot, everyone
who knows this voice:
I've fed off of you enough now.
It's time to send me packing.

Leave me no muses,
or just the ones who hold me
in contempt, who insist I never
write another line.

My touch bruises.
I can't look without coveting,
can't speak without wanting you
to hear me speak again.

If you know what's good for us,
what's good at all, run the other way.

2 p.m. Walk the dog

dragon

every day I hear a poem in the wind, every hour almost
and I forbid myself to write it down.
another will come, my heart says.
hold the poems lightly, my heart says, or they will grow big enough to eat you
they will eat your head; they will devour your heart raw out of your chest

every day I see poems in the branches of trees, caught, sodden, like plastic bags
and I forbid myself to extricate them
let the poems flutter out of the trees like music, my heart says, or they will eat you
they will pluck you off the walk like an eagle plucks out a salmon's eye

but here I am begging for another poem to blow like ashes into my eyes
to tangle claws in my hair — that when it drops it will be as a dragon
otherworldly, inexorable, belching flames and atom-bomb flowers
there I'd be underneath it, scrabbling to be its bull's-eye, its ground-zero princess

I tell myself there's just the sidewalk
merely two sneakers padding up the tree-lined hill; but the lie burns

in truth every pebble, every leaf, is a dragon sent to eat my juicy heart

glory **and** *rejoicing*

not a spotlight
  trained on you
but depth
  what is within
revealed

> *moss rejoices*
> *round the branches*
> *trails its veil's green corners*
> *in the stream*

not a halo
  like neon trembling in the tube
but an essence
  escaping rising
with warm-blooded heat

> *fern rejoices itself*
> *in its unfurling*
> *brown to green it spins and spreads*
> *days' imperceptible dancing*

not a corona placed
  on the head
but fire flaring
  from the guiseless glance

> *dandelions rejoice*
> *through the grass*
> *flat and gold as king's plates*
> *unashamed*

not a trumpet
  heralding
a red carpet
  unrolling
> *but a voice*
> *breathing love songs*
> *green and brown and golden*

no ugly people

all the hair in wings
sheets, clouds, falling
or sculpted, touchable
everyone with bath-shiny eyes
a sweep of lid or lash
cheekbones strong as a horse's brow

this planet is peopled
with perfectly kiss-sized chins
a world of solid jaws waiting
to be cupped, enfolded
between two hands

and anyone with a hand or two
is a moving masterpiece
no parcel of bones
more elegantly wired
more deft and delicate
with a zipper, a fork
the sticky pages of a book

not to mention the alliance
of hips, ankles, knees in a dance
and the backs of knees, kissed: human silk

in every square inch of us
beauty to stop your breath

poppy

wiry-stick-person
with a short mohawk, dyed orange
in a little flame at the forehead

wiry arms carrying a sorry-looking
dog, all its legs stuck straight out
from its fat brindled belly

wiry-stick-mohawk curled its arms
around that dog birth-tight, and walked
quickly, purposefully, down the cracked
old sidewalk. I wondered was the dog
sick? was it dead?

later, in the psychedelic tunnel
of fruits, flowers and flying seafood
in Pike Place Market, there was the dog:
alive and adoring, languid
at the feet of its master, wiry-stick-mohawk
who now clutches a small guitar
as thought it were her dog, sick or dead,
and tips up a beautiful, sharp-boned
singing face:
"*mariposa, mariposa, mariposa...*"

and the colour I mistook for hair dye
is a poppy, its wilted stem threaded
around a spike of hair, the flower head
heated by the heat of her singing head,
a little orange flame blooming
along her shaven skull.

I've never lived anywhere

only Vancouver

only the southeast
down the hill from little Kensington Park
from where the city tumbled and spilled
to the inlet, shining like a lode of mithril
and up out of the shine into dark mountains

the view from the park's top
a giant's vast, bejewelled belly print

only the west
late spring, greenblack nights in the basement suite
our honeymoon bed near the golf course
frogs on the endowment lands kept us awake
mating and mating

only south again
third floor, the old house with the tall windows
that you felt you could sail right out of
over Honest Nat's and the German deli
your feet touching down deliciously

now
looking back over Boundary Road
I live in Burnaby, green saddlebag
on Vancouver's eastern flank

my house just a warm box in the trees
between a highway and a salmon river

trains call in the night from way back east
to assure us that our place is not exotic
that all our wet and emerald days and nights
have been lived nowhere at all

3 p.m. Bring the children home from school

legit

Babies are landing in the world
from outside desire, and in the teeth of it,
every single one smaller and brighter,
more needy and exquisite,
than all our careful, condom-covered dreams.

Remember us: the unplanned children.
Some were *kept* (as the terminology goes)
and others *given up*, but every one of us
in the cloud of the word: *illegitimate*.

What makes a kid legit?

Breath, I figure. Sliding out
with a bloody hide and a squirm
and a good hard squall when they cut the cord.

Even before breath we qualified,
all of us swimming in the same sea.
The amniotic ship rose and fell
and had its own destination,
its own port of call — a harbour named light...

they did what they did, my sire and dam,
to stanch the bleeding, maybe, night bleeding
out their eyes and the ends of their overheated fingers
late summer pumping furiously through their skin
August pressing itself through them, pressing out

ever since the night my father's brave seed
smelled for just a microsecond the wet pacific air
and sailed away into the dark of my mother
in search of his mermaid, his siren
ever since that black-bright second
I've been *legitimate*

one small legitimate heartbeat
all the tiny legitimate DNA twirling
like plankton in all my baleen cells
I sailed like Jonah, my mission:
to be born.

a gift of tongues

Waiting in the lobby,
silent in the streams of three, no,
four languages, voices old and young,
a lovely syllabic sea.

The tiny girl on her father's lap
is speaking Cantonese in one long
preschool breath, sentences unending
like my son's, I imagine, punctuated
by a Chinese *and...and...and....*

Her small eyes are looking suddenly
at the ceiling and she says in English:
One
hundred
thousand
elephants!

A breath and she resumes
except for the fact

that her small spell has rippled
round the world.
Now every trunk is raised
in pachydermic glossolalia.
Every rheumy wrinkled eye praises.
Every elephant in the world, sweetheart,
now trumpets Cantonese.

a lightness dances

a lightness dances
a tangle of wet hair gathers
momentum; she cries
look mama, here's my cartwheel!
her limbs blur
whir in a gymnastic mist
and with a soft thump
resolve against the grass

splayed on the ground she laughs
and sighs, a snowless angel
my heavenless angel
I laugh and cry to see her
at night when she curls
suddenly long arms and legs
in futile fetal pose

because she's already born
we're all squeezed into daylight
against our will
together we squint at the sun
take baby steps
hold hands

she holds out her arms
begs I take her back in time
the sun keeps rising
suspended like a pendulum
counting our hours down

vacant lot, november

Who knows the joy of frost?
Who can calculate the fascination
of frozen grass bent in grey-green waves,
of walking with only its frictive sigh
and a slow sag, like walking on water?

The boy knows. The boy sees at once
a boat to row where the old log lies.
The dog knows. She finds under every sere leaf
a clue, a trace of the year's descending love.

They run ahead, that wood calling them,
and those clouds. The shadows between bushes
are the trails to exactly where they need to be.
That wood, dark and mum in the frozen air;
the path, made by coyotes in the night, for sure.
The dead trees, chilling. The yellow grass.

It all wears November's pall, a grey cast
that seems to inhale sound and exhale silence.
But a boy and a dog know this ruse, a game
November plays to coax them out, to winnow
his companions to the ones who love him best:

dashing in and out of the brambles, the spotted dog;
cheeks flushed, arms spread, eyes wide, the red-haired boy.

12

Beth murmurs from under the surface of sleep:
Where's Soft Bear?

The bear's bum up in the bed's corner
and I right him, slip him into her curled arms,
tuck the blankets under both their chins.

Everything's right in her world tonight,
two weeks from twelve years old.

Twelve says you get to stand at the top
of childhood's hill, look back and ahead
and it's all clear, a sunny summit, the grass emerald,
a delicious breeze and all your friends near at hand.

But twelve also says everything is going to change.
So before you head down the far side of that hill,
take a good look, Beth.
Hang on to Soft Bear and enjoy this quiet,
this softly snoring night.

what in our world gets bigger?

plates, mugs, cars, bottles of juice
if any of these got bigger
even imperceptibly, over time
we'd feel that the universe had been
left too long in the back of the fridge
that a foreign something
had invaded our brains, or the world

but when little people pop out
they begin it right away — they can't
keep their places — they grow

one summer your whole body, head to toe
will loll along your mother's torso
your always-surprised baby eyes
making a looking moon
of your half-head over her shoulder
your plump arm, draped down her arm,
no longer than a strand of spaghetti

a whole throbbing, thrumming self
contained in barely a lap

let ten years pass and that arm
can fling the car door open by itself
arms and legs of that self spill over
the biggest mother's arms
and his trunk is as big
as a young tree

bottles of cola rolling off
the assembly line do not do this,
they keep to their borders
don't expand their territory
don't begin to crowd us out
neither do favourite sweaters, shoes
neither do gold rings, the shower stall
or your seat on the bus

but we don't love those things, really
objects brought to a premature perfection
we love what grows and transmutes
arms and legs and always-staring eyes
spreading, unfolding toward an unseen end

5 p.m Make dinner while looking forward to the weekend

recipe

There is a path lined with rosemary,
        chives and sage, greens dark and light together,
and garlic's tapered fingers against the trellis.

There are her hands scented with rosemary.
        She's cut it, bundled, rinsed and twisted it,
wet on the board next to a warm lemon.

There are the silvery garlic skins
        in a fish-scale heap beside the knife,
and the cloves, the bed of garlic cloves in the pan.

Now there's the chicken stuffed with the rosemary
        and with the lemon, its skin all over pierced,
And the bird set down on the layer of garlic cloves.

There are her fingers in the olive oil,
        moving in small circles, spicing the skin
with cracked black pepper and crumbled rosemary.

There is the path lined with rosemary,
        chives and sage, and it's begun to rain.
There is the garlic, bending over by the trellis.

There she kneels, laying down the kitchen shears.
        There are her hands.

thursday sapphics

Evening calls from up in his onyx bedroom,
calls and lights his candle so we'll remember.
Morning keeps her hand on me, bright distraction:
                curtains of sunlight.

Afternoon, that breezy companion, knows me,
knows I'll dance the hours with him too quickly,
blocking out the backbeat, the thrum of evening,
                the stretching darkness.

Dinner a blur, our faces greedily gathering.
Laughing even at prayer, we hoard this hour.
Done, the chairs scrape an end and everyone scatters,
                fleeing the stillness.

Ambition threatens, beating us blue with hours.
Evening offers deliverance, a key to the prison.
Wander, wrapped in Evening's cloak, seeking nothing:
                stars and then sleep.

sky train, sunday morning

Fog.
Streetlights floating.
Five crows overhead in an arc.
All the dull chrome poles
leaning in the same direction.

Only the strained, high breathing
of the electromagnetic train
and a station's ribbed ceiling,
the inside of a whale.

A small bare wood; a siren.
Pigeons, a dozen little black bombs
out of the fog, chase the train.

On this side of the last station
everyone is a shade of grey
and the fog eats them in a minute.

On the other side the sun is rising.
The fog backs away. The leftover moon
is a narrow white breath
on blue.

stop reading that poetry book

and look up:
it's a summer morning
and the sliding SkyTrain
is a chapel of sunlight,
slanted buttresses, beaming
through the windows where it stains
shoulders, hair, cheekbones and the metal
bars into bright glass, into icing,
a light entirely rich and edible.

Just that one shoulder there, bare
and edged with gold along its bicep's black tattoo —
there is little else the morning need hold
to be called Sunday, to be called
a day of worship.

instructions for a day off

Wear your brightest, favourite clothes;
      wear blue and green; wear orange.

Run, if that's your wont, or walk slowly, feeling
      the whole sole of your shoe compress the grass.

Look at the dunes; look again, pausing
      for breath at every red and yellow flower.

Remember (how could you possibly forget?)
      the size of it – that continent of cloud.

Look for the wakes of fishing boats that send
      skirls of liquid glass along the sand.

When a thousand snow geese rise with a roar
      and a flickering off the distant delta, gasp.

Simple kites are best; eschew the complex.
      Fly the triangle and the long-tailed diamond.

The higher you let your kite ascend, the more
      the wind will clasp and carry it.

If you wait silently by the bird-filled grasses,
      you will see the cricket that you hear.

Keep standing, looking again at everything.
      Stay until sunset, until your legs ache.

Before you leave, build little cairns and nests
      among the boulders.

Write your names in the sand.

6 p.m. Greet spouse arriving home from work

juggling

This is our madness: we maintain.
We keep the hours in the air, many-coloured,
as though every one were meant
to be as merry as the last, the same smiles,
the same jokes,
the same lives propped-up together.

You pretend everything's the same,
as though we could suddenly live without gravity,
without earth under our feet. Without air.
It's really great to be here! you bellow,
expanding your chest as a sharp pain
begins in my breastbone
and the middle of my back.
I can see your frantic eyes,
but haven't breath enough to say a word.

You're juggling too, but I think you're better at it
than I am. You juggle the bright scarves of hours,
but years' knives too, and the single machete
of all our vows, spinning silver above your head.
In your hands it doesn't look life-threatening.
It looks somehow ordered;
every time you say *Love, I don't know,*
it turns into a shiny apple you can toss,
can take clever bites out of between passes.
I'm the volunteer from the audience:
smiling, but abashed. Secretly praying
for it all to be over with as little humiliation
as possible.

You position me,
slip a lit cigarette between my lips, steady me
in your sights as you draw back your arm.

after all these years I finally get to be the French Lieutenant's Woman

At last you've found your way to me,
joined me on this promontory
through our particular kind of darkness,
the one that leaves room for fingers
groping along the flagstones.

For so long you waited for me
to come back from the far end
of things, to get my fill
of the thrashing ocean, shadows of ships,
the almost adulterous caress of mist.

I know you were watching.
Feet planted firmly on the Victorian ground,
hob-nailed boots well-polished
and new, you kept coming back,
kept coming
just close enough to see whether or not
I'd been swept away.

Don't budge, I told myself.
He'll drag you back into his world,
a fall headlong into straight streets
and corsets, fossils packed into a canvas bag,
destined for the display case.
And when the wind was bad, and the dark
especially, it was tempting — without a word
he'll receive you. Press you
into his jigsaw life in a trice.
Morning would come then. Fog suddenly
white and the wind with its hands

around my ribcage. Another day in the middle
of this rushing, the sea's perpetual grey struggle.
Keep still.

So I was when I heard you approach:
fixed, a pillar at the swirling edge.

After so long looking out I turned my head,
your shadow creeping closer,
boots scrape along the stones.
You finally open your mouth,
call my name.

Now we're wet together. One hooded cape
covers us both. The wind has grown
more hands and balances us, parallel bodies
at the swirling edge.

We think of a warm house, a bed,
but the fog whitens. For one more morning
our cold hands press together
into the promontory's farthest stone.
We lean into the wind, into
the consummating caress of the mist.
Who knows? We may never come back
from the far end of things.

to husbands and wives

Find time to make love
in the day's middle.
The light is better.
Winter light through fog.
White light liquid and diffuse across your bodies.

Keep the curtains open. Yes,
the neighbours may get a glimpse.
Won't you *honour the marriage bed to keep it holy*
with a refracted second of your joy?

Cast off the dim years of doing it in the dark.
Let the watered light spread across your backs, your bellies.
In the history of all the world there has never
been a belly like that one. There never will be again.

Don't wait until night falls.
Now is the time. Kiss it.

7 p.m. Go out. Come home

waiting for the bus

After years in the cracked and uncracked streets,
at every stop within fifty miles your shade sits waiting for the bus.

It has made an art of waiting.
It has blocked entire plays at bus loops.
It has written an opera called *the secret glances of the fare-card holders*,
composed chamber music for the air brakes and the bells.

It has painted shelters with the coloured sweat of summer waiting;
built trolley buses from fallen leaves and ridden them over the trees;
transferred with disappearing slivers of ice; poured itself
into the fare box with the rain and with the coins danced itself silver.

It knows that the minutes before the bus are not barren,
that they are a gift of stillness, that they frame the journey.

Your shade is connected to the guy wires; your shade is powered by trolley; it is electric.
Its blue sparks rain down the years of cracked and uncracked streets.
It follows you, wires you up and fuels you, your footsteps turn the cities on.

gloss on lines by Dylan Thomas

By the sea's side, hearing the noise of birds,
Hearing the raven cough in winter sticks,
My busy heart who shudders as she talks
Sheds the syllabic blood and drains her words
        Dylan Thomas, "Especially when the October wind"

It's been too long since I have looked,
in the flesh, on the actual ocean, and walked
with my own two legs by the sea's side,
hearing the noise of birds flung down the air
like sharpened shells, like oysters bare, unpearled.

The past year was spent at dark intersections
with broken lights, breathing in weak clouds
near thin suburban woods, hearing the raven cough
in winter sticks his meagre dinner up.
His wings were wet asphalt; his eyes, street lamps.

Much shoe leather later and still no ocean
in sight. The traffic is crazy. I can keep
no real control of my busy heart who shudders
as she talks, trying to shake apart
her rusted call, her seized machinery.

I'll walk this wet black highway to the sea
because I know his physic for this ill:
he parts the breastbone, sheds the syllabic blood
and drains her words until the heart's a cup
he'll scour with waves, and with new pearls fill up.

a tiny girl behind heart's door

is peeking out
threatening to rejoice

the journey is on schedule:
the sun will be up another hour
there are empty chairs at the coffee bar

the tiny girl wants to dance a grateful jig
for one more slantlight evening
in this warm city

for the round man beside the bench
who loves his book — holds it in front of him
like a floppy brick and reads and reads

for the woman who wears
a long black tail of hair
and a bowler hat in the young evening

finally for a Joni Mitchell song
in the air   her *clean white linen*
her silken voice the spread sideways light
at five minutes to seven on a Wednesday in May

the tiny girl has her foot in the door
is determined to cross the threshold
and drag the dark heart out
someday soon the light will strike her
sharp, will bring to fruition
all her threats to cry for joy.

Meunier's "Prodigal Son"

after seeing the bronze by the Belgian sculptor

he kneels between his father's own spread knees
his body flung like a robe at the old man's heart

there son and father are transfixed, their stare
so solid it might be of some invisible bronze

all the ages of his son's life are thrown at this father
the young man, yes, longs arms, legs and stomach
taut-muscled even in surrender

but also, kneeling, the child too
looking up, soft-mouthed, into his father's eyes
for help and love — holding on
the small beseeching boy

as the father sees too the first long-ago sight
this father's long brown hands cup
the upturned head, cradle it as they gaze
as though his boy's neck were slack
as though his son were newly born

the shoes I wore in Naples

The shoes I wore in Naples
are in the seagrass basket I sent
back with you, along with the sausage,
the oil, and the little bottle of sand
I scooped up from the beach.

The many shells hurt my feet
so I couldn't go down to the water.
You looked down at me, your eyes
shining like pieces of beach glass,
rough-edged, pale amethyst.

It's time for us to leave this country.

Though I could barely hear you
(our nattering friends crowded around,
and the fireworks),
I knew you were right.

Above the fireworks a half-moon hung,
engorged, sliced exactly,
its dark twin hidden forever.

someday

I will call Cassiopeia out of the late summer sky
and show you her tipped "w", her two cupped hands, her two black breasts
(a torso draped across the constellations; you think that's only Andromeda.
No! it's Cassiopeia's long body too, leg bones tipped silver and spread,
remembering this attitude of birth: making way for her daughter).

Someday I will show you Cassiopeia at rest,
her tipped "w"; her two cupped hands; her two black breasts
slack and sparkling in space; the queen has retired,
lain on her throne; she has swept aside her robe of country stars;
has shown you her beauty in the sparse city night; has granted you an audience.

Someday when I show you Cassiopeia
you will mark her tipped "w"; you will ready your palms to catch what she drops
from her cupped hands; you will long for her black breasts.
She lies until the end in tipped, zigzag repose, eager to stretch the bent hands,
waiting to raise her breasts with each languid, starry breath.

What will you do when I show you Cassiopeia?
Will you see the first heaven crammed with ancient promises,
kings and queens and beasts in the almost black, lines
tracing the stars, lines that might be words or hands or breasts?

staying up

When you finally draw back the day's last blankets
there will be knowledge; enlightenment; silence
that bears meaning; music in the silver spheres.
And you will hear it this time, really, if you'll just
stay awake for ten more minutes.

Just ten more minutes and the lassitude will lift.
You'll get your second wind; the moon
will peel off her lamé balloon dress
and roll right on to your balcony, crooning.

sleep

The horizontal glory of the body, heavy, semiconscious, its whole surface pressing mattress and unmoving air.

The stillness of pillowed hair.

The moment before sleep, when you can see into its underground canal, its warm depths.

Hitting the surface, you grow sleep's gills and for the night you are his fish, a creature from above made wet now through and through.

For surely sleep will have his way with you.

Swimming under every night, under every sky, submerged yet living, the choiceless life of dreams where all you know is how the water pulls.

Dreams are the mer-people.

You envy them their meaty tails, their sleek silence and the chaste movements of long hair over breasts.

This is their native land and you are only a night visitor; a darker fish.

They let you believe, while you are here, that you are one of them, and that your legs, awkward as peeled sticks, will never return.

They imply that you will get to keep your gills,

but like the poor mermaid who peddled away her voice, you will be bare and two-legged in the morning.

You will long for your fish life. You will stumble up the beach and hope that the folk in the castle will take pity on you.

Your gills are gone.

Spread across a pillow, you feel your still hair.

The body, suddenly heavy, presses a mattress and unmoving air.

The hours' epilogue

friday: overwhelmed.

Would the moon plummet to earth
if today I did nothing of any earthly good?
Returned no calls, no letters,
bought nothing I need (admitting I probably don't need it)
and ate fruit and bread; drank milk.
Would the stars shatter if I cooked nothing?

Because, God in Heaven, the fleas of detail
are charging by the dozen up my unshaven legs.
Those locusts, the thousand trivial tasks, have arrived,
a plague of voracious jaws, and here I wait:
a shivering stand of wheat they'll cut in a minute.

So today I abdicate. Live in the mess;
Get yourself an apple from the fridge.
Come and lie with me on the unmade bed
until the moon rises where she's always been.

Diane Tucker was born and raised in Vancouver, British Columbia, where she got a B.F.A. from the University of B.C. in 1987. Nightwood Editions published her first book of poems, *God on His Haunches*, in 1996. It was shortlisted for the 1997 Gerald Lampert Memorial Award. Her poetry has been published in several anthologies and appears regularly in journals in Canada and abroad. Diane lives in Burnaby, British Columbia with her husband, her teenage daughter and son and Doxa the spotty dog.